HISPANIC LEADERS OF COURAGE

LIN-MANUEL MIRANDA

EZRA E. KNOPP

PowerKiDS press™

Published in 2026 by The Rosen Publishing Group, Inc.
2544 Clinton Street, Buffalo, NY 14224

First Edition

Editor: Therese Shea
Book Design: Michael Flynn

Photo Credits: Cover, p. 1 lev radin/Shutterstock.com; (series background) Sergei Mishchenko/Shutterstock.com; p. 5 DFree/Shutterstock.com; p. 7 lev radin/Shutterstock.com; p. 9 Debby Wong/Shutterstock.com; p. 11 Fred Duval/Shutterstock.com; p. 13 WENN Rights Ltd/Alamy Stock Photo; p. 15 Blueee77/Shutterstock.com; p. 17 Kathy Hutchins/Shutterstock.com; p. 19 AP Photo/Carlos Giusti; p. 21 Photo Win1/Shutterstock.com.

Library of Congress Cataloging-in-Publication Data

Names: Knopp, Ezra E., author.
Title: Lin-Manuel Miranda / Ezra E. Knopp.
Description: Buffalo : PowerKids Press, 2025. | Series: Hispanic leaders of courage | Includes index.
Identifiers: LCCN 2024044655 (print) | LCCN 2024044656 (ebook) | ISBN 9781499451108 (library binding) | ISBN 9781499451092 (paperback) | ISBN 9781499451115 (ebook)
Subjects: LCSH: Miranda, Lin-Manuel, 1980–Juvenile literature. | Composers–United States–Biography–Juvenile literature. | Lyricists–United States–Biography–Juvenile literature. | Actors–United States–Biography–Juvenile literature.
Classification: LCC ML3930.M644 K56 2025 (print) | LCC ML3930.M644 (ebook) | DDC 782.1/4092 [B]–dc23/eng/20240920
LC record available at https://lccn.loc.gov/2024044655
LC ebook record available at https://lccn.loc.gov/2024044656

Manufactured in China

Some of the images in this book illustrate individuals who are models. The depictions do not imply actual situations or events.

CPSIA Compliance Information: Batch #QSPK26. For Further Information contact Rosen Publishing at 1-800-237-9932.

CONTENTS

Many Talents

Lin-Manuel Miranda is a **composer**, writer, rapper, and actor. He's best known for his **musical** *Hamilton*. It is about U.S. history, but told through hip-hop music. It was unlike anything before it. People loved it—and still do! *Hamilton* is just one of Miranda's many successes.

Childhood

Lin-Manuel Miranda was born January 16, 1980, in New York City. His parents, Luz and Luis, are from Puerto Rico. The family lived in Inwood, New York City, a mostly Hispanic neighborhood. Young Lin-Manuel's life included both Hispanic and American **customs**.

Luz Towns-Miranda
Luis A. Miranda Jr.

Miranda listened to many kinds of music. He loved hip-hop and **Broadway** musicals. He took piano lessons and sang in groups too. Miranda spoke Spanish at home and English at school. He spent a month each summer in Puerto Rico. But sometimes he felt like he didn't belong wherever he was.

Getting on Stage

Miranda began taking part in musicals in middle school. Finally, he felt like he belonged! He loved **performing**. He also started writing stories and music. In college, he studied movies and plays. He began to write a musical. It was about a New York City neighborhood like his own.

In the Heights

After college, Miranda was offered a job as a teacher. But he knew he loved the theater world. He made a brave choice. He chose to continue to write his musical. In 2008, Miranda's musical, *In the Heights*, opened on Broadway. It won many awards, or honors.

PLAYBILL

Hamilton

In 2008, Miranda read a book about **Founding Father** Alexander Hamilton. He began to compose a musical about Hamilton. He used hip-hop and other kinds of music. He asked **diverse** actors to play the main roles. In 2015, *Hamilton* opened on Broadway. Miranda starred. It was a huge hit and won many awards.

HAMILTON
AN AMERICAN MUSICAL
BY
LIN-MANUEL MIRANDA

On to Disney

The Walt Disney Company asked Miranda to write songs for the 2016 movie *Moana*. He starred in the movie *Mary Poppins Returns* in 2018. He also composed music in English and Spanish for the 2021 movie *Encanto*. In 2023 and 2024, Miranda had a role on the Disney TV show *Percy Jackson and the Olympians*.

Working for Puerto Rico

Miranda says his Puerto Rican roots are a part of everything he does. In 2017, the storm called Hurricane Maria landed on Puerto Rico. Many people were killed, and buildings were destroyed. Miranda raised money to help the people there.

Connecting Kids to the Arts

Lin-Manuel Miranda has many other causes too. Some schools don't have music or theater programs. He's trying to change that. In 2022, he gave many musical **instruments** to New York City high schools. Miranda is a leader on stage and off!

A Leader in Music and More

1980

Lin-Manuel Miranda is born January 16 in New York City.

1999

Miranda starts to write *In the Heights* in his second year of college.

2008

In the Heights opens on Broadway.

2015

Hamilton opens on Broadway.

2016

Moana, a Disney movie with Miranda's music, comes out.

2018

He has a role in *Mary Poppins Returns*.

2021

The movie *Encanto* features Miranda's music.

2022

Miranda receives the Changemaker Award for his work in the arts and for people in need.

GLOSSARY

Broadway: A street in New York City with many theaters. Also, the world of the theater in that city.

composer: Someone who writes music.

custom: An action or way of acting commonly practiced by a group of people or in a place.

diverse: Describing people different from each other.

Founding Father: One of the men who had an important role in creating the U.S. government.

instrument: An object used to make music.

musical: A play that uses singing, music, and dancing to tell a story.

perform: To play music or sing.

FOR MORE INFORMATION

BOOKS

Gaston, Stephanie. *Lin-Manuel Miranda.* New York, NY: Crabtree Publishing, 2023.

Matos, Elijah Rey-David. *Who Is Lin-Manuel Miranda?* New York, NY: Penguin Workshop, 2024.

Rose, Rachel. *Lin-Manuel Miranda: Composer, Singer, and Actor.* Minneapolis, MN: Bearport Publishing, 2022.

WEBSITES

Lin-Manuel Miranda
kids.britannica.com/kids/article/Lin-Manuel-Miranda/633689
Read more about his life and work.

Lin-Manuel Miranda
www.linmanuel.com
Find out more about Miranda's latest news on his website.

INDEX